爱迪生

Heroes and Role Models | Non-Fiction Series

Copyright © 2022 by Level Learning, INC. and Washington Yu Ying PCS™

Original and Edited Text Copyright © 2022 by Washington Yu Ying PCS™

All rights reserved. No part of this book in whole or part may be reproduced without written permission from the publisher.

Published by Level Learning, INC.

Content Contributors:
Washington Yu Ying PCS™
Level Learning - Ya-Ching Chang

Illustrations by: Josh Taira

Leveling classification based on Level Learning standard. For full description, visit www.levellearning.com

ISBN 978-1-64040-000-9
*Simplified Chinese Edition*

**About Level Learning:**
Level Learning provides a literacy focused curriculum specifically designed for K-12 Chinese as a Second Language classrooms. Our program offers 20 levels of specific and detailed objectives, leveled texts and passages, mastery-based online assessment, and analytics to enable data-driven instruction. Level Learning reading curriculum for both literature and informational text emphasize grammar and comprehension skills to help teachers develop confident and independent Chinese language readers. The non-fiction series of books are specifically designed to support our informational text course based on multiple national standards. To learn more about our entire offering, visit www.levellearning.com.

**About Washington Yu Ying PCS™:**
Washington Yu Ying PCS is a Mandarin English dual language immersion International Baccalaureate (IB) World school. Yu Ying's mission is to inspire and prepare young people to create a better world by challenging them to reach their full potential in a nurturing Chinese/English educational environment. Yu Ying's comprehensive IB, dual immersion curriculum equips students with global competencies for success in the real world. As a leader in immersion education, Yu Ying is determined to advance Chinese language programs and global citizenry education by helping other schools create and strengthen their Chinese programs. For more information, email: products@washingtonyuying.org

爱迪生是美国著名的发明家，出生于1847年。他从小就有非常强的好奇心，常常问一些奇怪的问题，有时候大人们都不知道这些问题的答案。

因为爱迪生喜欢在学校不停地问问题，这让老师很头疼，所以他只上了十二个星期的小学，就留在家里一边和妈妈学习一边做实验。在这段时间里，爱迪生不仅学习了大量的知识，而且也有了更多时间做他感兴趣的科学实验。

做实验需要买大量的材料，而且有些材料也不便宜。对于一个小孩子来说，这毫无疑问是一件困难的事情。为了有足够的钱做实验，在十二岁的时候，爱迪生开始在火车上卖糖果和报纸。他把这些钱都存下来，用于做实验。

就这样，爱迪生在各种科学实验中长大了。长大后的爱迪生更加明确了自己的目标。他盖了一间实验室，和他的同事在里面发明了很多东西。电灯就是其中一个发明。

在发明电灯以后，爱迪生又发明了一个电力系统，让电灯泡可以发光。那时的他还不知道，就是这个小小的电灯泡，对全世界的人们都有着非常重要的意义。

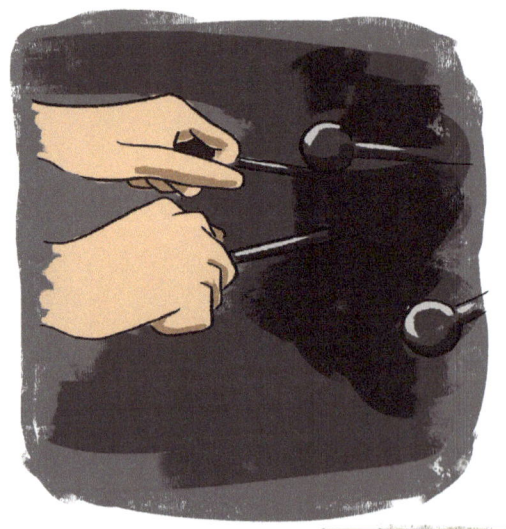

1882年的一天,爱迪生打开了一个开关,给纽约的85间房子带来光亮。这是人类历史上第一次使用电灯照明。从此以后,夜晚也因为这些光亮变得更加美丽。

除了电灯以外,爱迪生还有一千多项发明。爱迪生的发明,改变了我们的世界,也改善了我们的生活。

# Glossary

|  | Pinyin | English Definition |
|---|---|---|
| 著名 | zhù míng | famous |
| 发明家 | fā míng jiā | inventor |
| 好奇心 | hào qí xīn | curious |
| 头疼 | tóu téng | headache |
| 大量 | dà liàng | a lot of |
| 知识 | zhī shi | knowledge |
| 感兴趣 | gǎn xìng qù | interested |
| 科学实验 | kē xué shí yàn | science experiment |
| 材料 | cái liào | material |
| 便宜 | pián yi | cheap |
| 毫无疑问 | háo wú yí wèn | no doubt |
| 足够 | zú gòu | enough |
| 存 | cún | to save |
| 目标 | mù biāo | goal |
| 实验室 | shí yàn shì | laboratory |

|  | Pinyin | English Definition |
|---|---|---|
| 电力系统 | diàn lì xì tǒng | power systems |
| 意义 | yì yì | meaning, consequence |
| 开关 | kāi guān | generator |
| 照明 | zhào míng | light, illumination |
| 改变 | gǎi biàn | to change |
| 改善 | gǎi shàn | to improve |

www.ingramcontent.com/pod-product-compliance
Lightning Source LLC
Chambersburg PA
CBHW041226070526
44584CB00001B/111